, 495

"You Can Tell Your Kid Will Grow Up To Be A Librarian When. . ."

"You Can Tell Your Kid Will Grow Up To Be A Librarian When. . ."

Cartoons About The Profession
by Richard Lee

McFarland & Company, Inc., Publishers
Jefferson, North Carolina & London

The following cartoons have been previously published in *American Libraries:* page 24 (October 1991), page 31 bottom (June 1992) and page 45 top (January 1988). The cartoon on page 44 appeared in the *Las Vegas Sun* (April 23, 1989).

British Library Cataloguing-in-Publication data are available

Library of Congress Cataloguing-in-Publication Data

Lee, Richard.
    You can tell your kid will grow up to be a librarian when . . . :
cartoons about the profession / Richard Lee.
      p. cm.
    ISBN 0-89950-743-3 (sewn softcover : 55# alk. paper) ∞
    1. Libraries—United States—Caricatures and cartoons.
2. American wit and humor, Pictorial. I. Title.
Z682.5.L44 1992
020′.207—dc20   92-50309
                                            CIP

Manufactured in the United States of America

McFarland & Company, Inc., Publishers
 Box 611, Jefferson, North Carolina 28640

Acknowledgments

Thank you! Thank you! A thousand times thank you to all of my friends who helped in the conception and creation of this, my first book. A special thanks goes to a really great group at the Las Vegas-Clark County Library District: Cynthia, Mike, Shelley, Phyllis, Jan, and Rocky.

I lovingly dedicate this work to my wife, Laurie, my daughter Rena, my son Andy, and to my parents, Gene and Jeanette.

To you, who shell out $14.95, enjoy!

Table of Contents

Acknowledgments   v

Foreword by Cynthia Gaffey   ix

Kids Who Will Grow Up To Be Librarians   1

Parents Who Are Librarians   9

The Reference Desk   17

People Who Love The Profession   24

About Patrons & Books   39

Library Fauna (Text by Mike Bisceglia)   49

Library Trading Cards   60

The Ins & Outs of Library School   66

The Dos & Don'ts of ALA Committee

    Participation   81

My Story (Text by Mike Bisceglia)   85

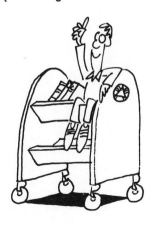

Foreword

On first meeting, Richard Lee's choir boy quality comes through, that sincere innocence in his face and manner. He's a librarian, and seems to be serious about his work. His love of baseball soon comes out; and that rounds out an all-American boy image. Later it dawns that the light in his eye is actually the glint of mischief and that his smile may in fact be a smirk.

Then one realizes that Richard looks at things in a dual way. In reality, he's a cartoonist who only happens to be a librarian, and although he's serious about librarianship, he's checking each situation for a gag. Currently he runs the Clark County Detention system library--the jail library-- for the Las Vegas-Clark County Library District and his education includes a bachelor's degree from Minnesota and a Master's degree in library science from Brigham Young University. Richard has also worked for Dynix, a major library automation company.

The library world, seen through Richard's eyes, provides a rich field of humor. His point of view lightens the vexations which librarians know so well, such as the aggravations of library school or the frustrations of working on a public service desk. But his humor often takes an imaginative, whimsical turn away from literal workaday situations, such as in the series "You Can Tell Your Kid Will Grow Up To Be A Librarian When..." In it, Richard exposes the quirks of librarians' pre-pubescent years.

Apart from his slant on library life, much of the humor in his cartoons comes from a mature, well-developed drawing style. The laughs are in the lines he draws. His characters look funny. The expressions on their faces often reveal the joke before you read the gag line. The way he draws a broken-down bookmobile is inherently funny.

Richard developed his knack for cartooning on his own beginning in 1974, then honed his craft with guidance from a semester of art classes at Utah State. The cartooning bug first bit when, as a lad in the Midwest, he looked at cartoons in farm journals and figured he could cartoon at least that well and probably better. He was proven right when he began to draw and submit cartoons to periodicals which purchased and published them. By now, his cartoons, not always on the subject of libraries, have been published in major magazines, including such venerable library publications as American Libraries and Wilson Library Bulletin. Richard is the first to say that the publications which have rejected his cartoons are at least as distinguished as those which have accepted.

He now cartoons on a drafting table at home and considers it a business, not just a lucrative hobby. And he relies on the tolerance of his family in his cartooning, often using his son and daughter as models for his sketches to get a body position or hand just right. But he indicates that stock hand-on-hip and rolled-eyes look of exasperation may in fact have been taken from life and not posed.

When he's on a roll, he can work up 20 gags in just a couple of days, but he points out that the flow can dwindle to a precious few when he suffers from writer's block. That writer's block is not evident in "You Can Tell Your Kid Will Grow Up To Be A Librarian When ... "—a delightful cartoon excursion into libraryland and the imagination of Richard Lee.

Cynthia Gaffey
Community Relations Coordinator
Las Vegas-Clark County Library District

Kids are strange. Kids are
influenced by their
parents, their peers,
and their environment.
But some kids are stranger
than others. Their actions
are hard to explain or just
don't seem logical.
That's why
' You Can Tell Your
Kid Will Grow Up
To Be A Librarian
When ... '

...he makes dumb trades.

1

Kids

...he spells weird things with his blocks.

...her Christmas list is unabridged, annotated,
and alphabetized.

...she is generous with her toys but requires their prompt return in two weeks.

3

...she always out lasts you every night you read her a bedtime story.

Kids

...she classifies her meals by substance and content.

4

...he can't quite get the hang of team sports.

...her bath toys take on a whole new look.

...she'd rather arrange the cookbooks than learn to cook.

Kids

...she'd rather go to the school library than dissect frogs in biology class.

6   ...she is easily bribed by older siblings.

...he's always shushing strangers.

7

...his book reports go on forever.

Kids

"Go to the library, go to the library,
can't you kids watch TV like other kids!?"

"Someday, son, this will all be yours."

Parents

10

Parents don't come with a set of instructions. Sometimes their methods are inexplicable, but you can always tell when your parents are librarians because. . .

. . . on vacation, they take your picture in front of dull buildings.

Parents

... they bring you dumb presents from goofy conferences

... they tattle tape everything in the house.

. . . their idea of helping you on your paper route is creating a database of paid & unpaid subscribers.

. . . you always know when banned books week is.

13

Parents

...their CD player only plays stuff like 'Psych Lit'&
'Dissertation Abstracts'.

. . . when you're home sick from school, one of them
stays with you and reads from the current PDR.

... the only stats your Dad is interested in are title fill rates & books per capita.

15

... their coffee table books spill over to other pieces of furniture and major appliances.

Parents

. . . they form committees to discuss household mundane tasks like 'WASTE BASKET CONTENT REMOVAL PROCEDURES.'

. . . they make you take down your cool posters and put up ALA stuff.

Reference work. We all recall being told that whenever possible, take the patron to the stacks and don't point. Well. . .sometimes we're just too swamped! For those busy times when you simply cannot leave the desk, I offer these creative pointing techniques.

WHEN THEY ASK FOR:

an Elvis biography.

17

Reference Desk

WHEN THEY ASK FOR:
'hunting' magazines.

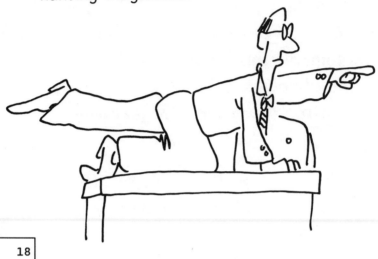

WHEN THEY ASK FOR:
aerobic exercise videos.

WHEN THEY ASK FOR:

books on acting.

19

WHEN THEY ASK FOR:

any historical information on the

Napoleonic War.

Reference Desk

WHEN THEY ASK FOR:
a sports officiating handbook.

WHEN THEY ASK FOR:
musical scores.

WHEN THEY ASK FOR:
Fine arts books.

WHEN THEY ASK FOR:
Political science texts.

Reference Desk

WHEN THEY ASK FOR:
Anything on Star Trek.

WHEN THEY ASK FOR:
Books on air traffic controlling.

23

"Of course the Farmer's Almanac is a fine publication Leroy, however you cannot answer every reference question using that one tool alone."

"It seems to be an early Reader's Guide
to Periodical Literature."

The Profession

"A driver's license, birth certificate, major credit cards, and a passport are all well and good Sir, but to cash a check in this bank I really need to see a library card."

27

"Oh Wilbur and I had a great cruise. I read
<u>Sands of Time</u> on the beach at Mazatlan,
<u>Chances</u> in an adorable little cabana in
Puerto Vallarta, and <u>Once in a Lifetime</u>
while sightseeing in Acapulco."

"Yes, ah, come in Randy. I have a shelf check for <u>Friends Apart</u> by Philip Toynbee."

29

"It's a what?"

The Profession

LIBRARIANS AT A LOVERS' LANE

The Profession

31

REFERENCE

SECOND OPINIONS

"Of course the 49ers and the Giants are important, but we're discussing the symbolism of Thomas Mann."

"That's Batson, he's a librarian
during the off season."

The Profession

"...and do you, Larry, take Ruth, in sickness and in health, for rich or for poor, and all her unresolved library fines?"

34

"Oh I'm not here to see the Doctor.
I come in once a month to weed his collection."

The Profession

"The Harlequin Romances are in the vending machine in the lobby next to the Coke machine."

"I just began my search and all of a sudden I was watching Wheel Of Fortune."

CONCERT PIANIST MEETS
ONLINE SEARCHER

37

"When I mentioned exit control, I meant perhaps targeting the collection."

"Let me get this straight. You can't remember the title or author, but it has a black & white cover?"

40

Sandy's love for books was
beginning to worry us.

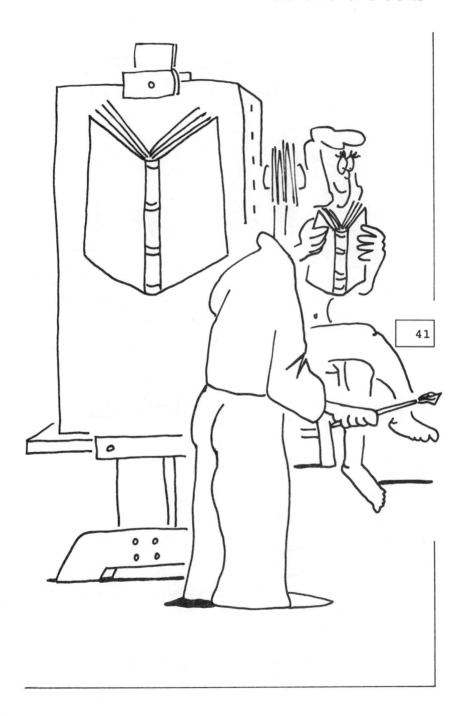

41

"Did the system die Arlene?"

43

"Well, it's a good book, certainly not a
great book . . . does it speak
to you young man?"

"Okay, that'll be due back in one to ten years."

"First all I had to do was fetch his evening paper, now I gotta run down to the library and pick out some contemporary fiction for him."

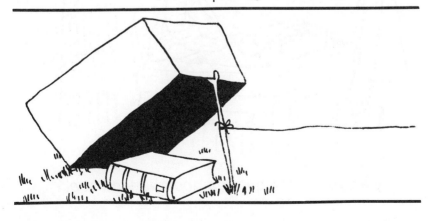

Patrons & Books

"Short stories?"

"Can you recommend a good banned book?"

"Mr. Faye doesn't care that the
computer says it's on the shelf.
Mr. Faye says it's not on the shelf.
Mr. Faye wants to know if you're going
to believe him or the computer?"

"It's just weird. I've looked and looked but that Amelia Earhart biography has just vanished."

LIBRARY FAUNA

Unlike other locales, which are the natural habitats for America's wildlife, this nation's libraries are the domains of several breeds of human fauna. Library observers are uncertain if these various strains are drawn to this realm because of the non-threatening conditions or because of mysterious symbiotic attractions these individuals have for one another.

This booklet is an attempt to identify only a minute number of the most unusual species found in many libraries. Casual observers of library fauna are encouraged to use this guide as a reference tool. Please do NOT attempt to make actual contact with any observed species. Although these species may appear tame in most instances, actual contact should be made by a trained professional...your local librarian.

Text by Mike Bisceglia

49

Library Fauna

FOUL WEATHER PATRON
(rainius orsnowius goindoorius)

This patron only appears when weather is other than fair, or if he missed the bus. If too hot, or too cold, or too wet, this patron appears until either the weather clears or until closing time. Easily identified by an open newspaper over his head, this patron is always amazed by how much the library has changed since his last visit.

Call: "What happened to the towel dispenser in the rest room? All I see is a blower in there."

IRATE PATRON
(madasus ahatterus)

An uncommon species, although easily identified by a scarlet face and large purple veins standing out in the neck. Chiefly found at circulation desks, although occasionally located at reference areas. Usually becomes agitated if book sought is unavailable.

Call: "#$^*!*#@ + !!"

Library Fauna

SLEEPER
(catnapeus publicus)

These patrons are noted for their inability to keep their eyes open. They can be found sleeping on shelves, napping in nooks, snoozing on floors, snoring on tables, or dozing at the microfiche.

Call: "Sleeping? I was just resting my eyes."

53

STACK LOUNGER
(readius all over the placeius)

A species noted for total concentration and a weak spine. Is known to arrive at a library before the doors are open and is the last to leave. Usually begins to read while seated in a chair or on a stool and will gradually slide onto the floor. Voracious literary appetite. Has been known to build a book cocoon in an aisle of adult fiction.

Call: "Hmm? Oh, sure! I'm ready to go. Could you help me up? My legs seem to have fallen asleep."

Library Fauna

54

YELLOW BELLIED SNEAK THIEF
(takeus anythingeus notnaileddowneus)

The THIEF comes in all ages, sizes, shapes, and from all social strata. He can be identified by the constantly shifting eyes and the curious bulges under his clothing. No object in the library is too small or too large for the THIEF. He is prepared for flight at the slightest hint of trouble.

Call: "I have no idea how those encyclopedias found their way into my pockets."

EVER EATER
(omnivorius anytimeius anyplaceius)

Usually seen entering with one or more large grocery bags. These individuals have a knack of disappearing into the recesses of the library. When located, they can usually be found amid a small ocean of food wrappings and soda cans. They have a curious habit of decorating the underside of tables with large wads of gum.

Call: "Mrpph hygrath isth murwtph thnk thoos boks!"

Library Fauna

CUTE KID
(eggheadius pa.ininth.eneckius)

Child, usually under the age of 16. Rarely found in the children's department. Often accompanied by a proud parent, the child is easily identified by the bulging attache case. He is a never-ending stream of questions for all librarians on duty. If the librarian does not have a ready answer, the child is frequently known to supply one. Any attempts to hide in a rest room are futile; the child will out wait you.

Call: "Tomorrow I would like to explore the imbalance in world trade and possibly seek viable answers to our nation's fossil fuel shortages."

57

VIGILANT VANDAL
(spraypaintius luminousius)

This first cousin of the SNEAK THIEF is
ever watchful for the opportunity to spray
paint a wall, carve his initials in a desk,
tear pages from a book, or cause
unremovable, unsightly spots in carpeting.
He, like the THIEF, can be found anywhere
in the library doing anything but reading a
book. The mature vandal is known to call:

Call: "Unbelievable! My taxes have
           gone up again!"

Library Fauna

58

PLOT TELLER
(totalstoryius relateius)

This individual can be found primarily around circulation desks at the busiest times. The PLOT TELLER always manages to find his way to the front of a long line of patrons wishing to check out their materials. Once at the counter, the TELLER will start telling other patrons about the plots in all of the books they are about to check out. He can be identified by very thick ankles and a slow moving departure.

Call: "Oh, another book you'll enjoy is...It's about..."

COLLECTION MOVER
(no payius that's okayius)

A singularly industrious species. Oblivious to the nesting arrangement of all materials in the library. Believes aesthetic alignment of texts to be more crucial than alphabetical order or Library of Congress classification. Has been known to arrange texts according to color, height or width. Is not seeking employment. Does not seek to be a volunteer.

Call: "Would you look at that! I put this section in order just yesterday and now someone has messed it all up again. Well, I certainly am going to be busy today."

What do baseball, Davy Crockett, hockey, Star Trek and the Beatles have in common? You're right! They all appear in sets of trading cards. But, just when you thought you had every conceivable set of every conceivable series ever printed, the hottest set yet appears on the horizon...LIBRARY CARDS.

60

Fred Crotts
BIBLIOGRAPHIC
INSTRUCTOR

Lefty Silver
ACQUISITIONS

Ruth Anne Lipitski
CIRCULATION

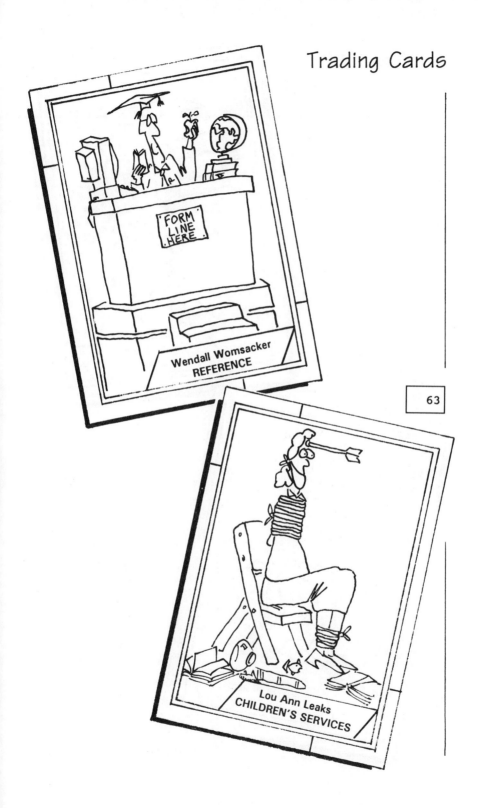

Trading Cards

Mary Kaye Fox
ILL

Harold Beasley
DIRECTOR

64

THE IN'S & OUT'S OF
LIBRARY SCHOOL

Some of us had trouble the first time we soloed with a book truck. Campus security could see we were inexperienced and often pulled us over to check our learner's permits.

In a book preservation seminar, we were taught to take every precaution in handling frail, antiquated volumes.

Library School

I took an elective course in bookmobiles. I expected to learn the organization, operation, and administration of this type of service but found the curriculum somewhat more basic.

I had a little trouble organizing my cataloging extra credit project. Boy am I glad they invented computerized catalogs.

69

Library School

The communication process was formally diagramed.

We were given modest lists of tools to memorize for reference class.

When I went to the University bookstore to purchase my textbooks, I was surprised to find other required materials. Then I had to explain over and over to the other students in line my class schedule.

71

Library School

In almost all of my classes, one basic philosophy seemed to continue to surface: Satisfy the patron's needs.

We had often been told about professional burnout, but until we had a chance to observe a severe case first hand, we had no idea how traumatic the condition could be.

Library School

The camaraderie of the faculty was touching. They often helped cheer one another up after spending long hours grueling over mounds of paperwork. I was amazed how often a professor with a double Masters and a Doctorate had trouble with tasks many of us took for granted like balancing a checkbook.

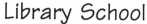

We learned about all
types of systematic
enumerative bibliographies.
Subject bibliographies,
analytical bibliographies,
textual bibliographies,
this bibliography,
that bibliography,
until...

75

Many of my classmates told me that as
undergrads they didn't take German, French, or
Spanish but something called SuDoc.

Library School

Many of my classmates took a children's services class which demanded they visit a preschool or day care and tell a story. They practiced for weeks and then finally suited up and ventured out to satisfy this requirement.

I practiced searching quickly and effectively with DIALOG and OCLC.

My first attempts to 'network' with my online remote database lab partner were frustrating.

At graduation, we learned the real value of our MLS when the keynote speaker told us about the coupon on the back of our diplomas that was good for $2 off the purchase of our next large two item pizza.

"Sorry Taylor, it's a new NCAA rule.
We're trading you to Northern State
for two history majors, a physics TA,
and an MLS candidate to be named later."

"Impressive resume, Miss Bramwell."

THE DO'S AND DON'TS OF ALA COMMITTEE PARTICIPATION

DO: Drink lots of water.

DO: Play with the pencils.

DO: Drink heavily the
    night before.

DO: Yawn a lot.

ALA Committees

DO: Check your watch a lot.

DO: Fall asleep.

DO: Drink more water.

DO: Stare blankly into space.

82

DO: Play some more with the pencils.

DO: Paw thru exhibitor freebies.

ALA Committees

DO: Arrive late.

DO: Leave early.

ALA Committees

DO: Yawn a lot more. DO: Blow interesting smoke rings.

THERE ARE ONLY TWO DON'TS.

DON'T: Look intelligent. ABOVE ALL, DON'T: Volunteer!

MY STORY

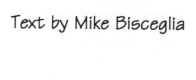

Text by Mike Bisceglia

My story is simple. I always wanted to be a baseball player. That's it, a baseball player. Not a fireman. Not a TV star. Not even an astronaut. And certainly not a librarian, just a baseball player.

My Story

I was born in a small town in America's heartland. A nice town. A simple town. A town with six little league fields. A town that was only fifty miles away from a big city with a real major league farm team. I lived in a great place.

My dad was a nice guy.
Not a great guy. Not a rich guy.
Not even a handsome guy, but a
nice guy. My dad was a library
administrator.

My Story

My mom was pretty neat too. She wasn't a great looking woman. She wasn't a great cook. She wasn't particularly witty. She was a reference librarian.

My Story

89

My dad and mom had great plans
for my future. They wanted me to
be... you guessed it, a librarian too.
Before I could walk, they
introduced me to the wonderful
world of books. Before I could talk,
I had my own library card.

My Story

But I dreamed only of baseball.

91

As a young boy, my dad taught
me all of the finer points of library
life. He showed me that when I
held my index finger up and pursed
my lips together, I could make
adults whisper, even when they
were already talking very low. Then
he showed me that when I put my
finger to my lips and said, "SHHH,"
I could make a whole reading room
full of kids almost swallow their tongues.

My Story

But I didn't want to hear quiet. I wanted to hear cheers. I wanted to be the second baseman who could turn a triple play to end the game. Let's face it, the smell of hot dogs in the open air is a lot more romantic than the smell of dusty old books in a building full of them.

When my dad was busy with a patron, my mom would take over my library education. She was a true artist when it came to checking out a patron's stack of books. Not only was she able to put the return date on the right line every time, she was fast... not as fast as a batter can scramble to first base after he lays down a good bunt, but she was fast.

93

My Story

94

The patrons loved her.

As I grew older, dad and mom
made me work in the library. I got
to be pretty good at shelving
books. I hardly ever shelved a
book incorrectly.

95

My Story

I knew, however, that my true talent lay not in the stacks but on the diamond. I was destined.

96

But dad and mom didn't want to know about my destiny. When I wanted to discuss the merits of the sacrifice fly, my mom wanted to explore the necessities of cataloging realia.

97

My Story

Dad took his place in the line-up right next to mom. When I wanted to discuss the needs for a proper pre-game warm-up, dad would show me that a library didn't run on books alone. Money was needed for everything, and sometimes it was hard to come by.

It was at those times that dad had to use all of his skills from logic to out-and-out begging to obtain the funds he needed.

99

My Story

When it was too embarrassing to be around dad, mom would make sure I understood that if dad struck out it would be a real major league loss and not just a pre-season scrimmage. My mom had a very strong influence on my life.

During those "fund" times, a patron might drag dad through a question negotiation. I thought my dad would be about ready to lose it. He would remind me of a manager with no left-hander to put on the mound to close the game.

My Story

Those were scary times. Even my great daydreams of our national pastime, in which I was always the hero, were in serious trouble. I remember once dreaming that I was about to march out to the on-deck circle, and dad was strolling onto the field right beside me... reading The Fund Raiser's Guide. What a nightmare!

103

Then one day it happened. My two favorite teams in the whole world, the Walla Walla Wombats and the Oshkosh Owls, were going to play an exhibition game in the big city only fifty miles from my home!

My Story

I told dad that I wanted to go the game. Uh-uh. I told dad that I needed to go to that game. No luck. Then, using the tried and true business tactics I had learned from dad, I begged him to take me to the game. Unbelievably, it worked!

So, off to the game we went.
And what a beautiful day for the
game it was. The crowds filled the
stadium, and I brought my glove
along just in case. Catching a
home run ball was like finding an
answer. And if there's one thing I
learned in the library, you can't
find the answer unless you have
the proper tools.

105

106

I had to admit, however, that the
chances of catching a home run
ball seated three sections up in
deep center field seemed highly
remote. No one could ever accuse
my dad of wasteful spending.

My Story

It was a classic game. Outstanding pitchers faced overpowering batsmen. Singles, doubles, and triples were sprinkled throughout the first eight innings, but still not a run had crossed the plate.

107

My Story

Then in the ninth inning, it happened. My eyes were glued to the plate. My favorite player for the Wombats, Tug McCord, was at bat. I imagined myself as Tug looking out to the mound and seeing Willie "The Whip" Williams of the Owls unleashing his feared fastball. Williams went into his wind-up and then came the pitch. The hit. That ball was headed my way! It was a home run ball and it was headed to me.

It was my big chance. My moment in the sun. My future as a baseball player was about to begin! I raised my hand. Stuck out my glove and... I missed. But the ball didn't miss me!

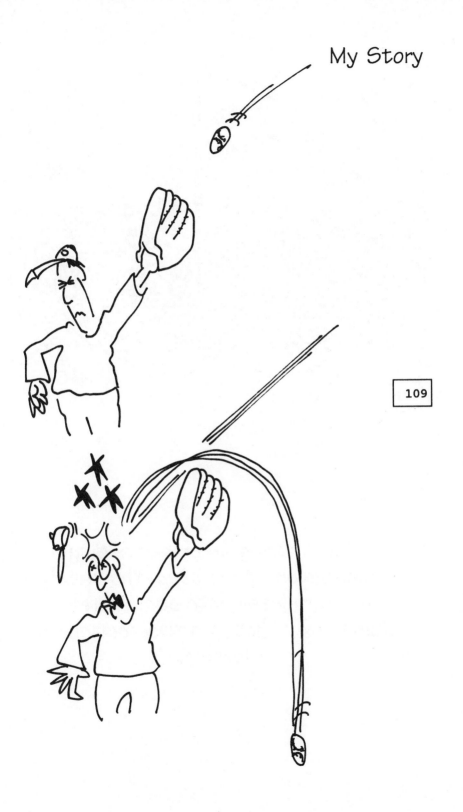

My Story

My Story

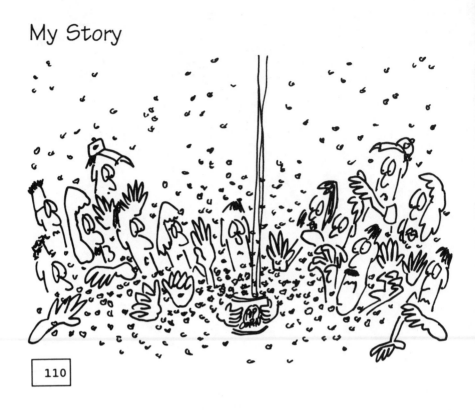

After making an embarrassing impression on my head, the ball fell harmlessly into some kid's dumb box of popcorn two sections below me.

After offering menacing glances
to the players gathered around
home plate some 470 feet away
and stern looks to the fans
seated below us, my dad tried to
cheer me up with memorable
quotes and unforgettable
sayings. It didn't help.

My Story

So, the next day it was back to library biz. Instead of dreams of racing to the plate, I was meandering down aisles of books. And instead of celebrating a postgame victory and dreaming of big league contracts, I was stuffing crummy old books back on the shelves.

112

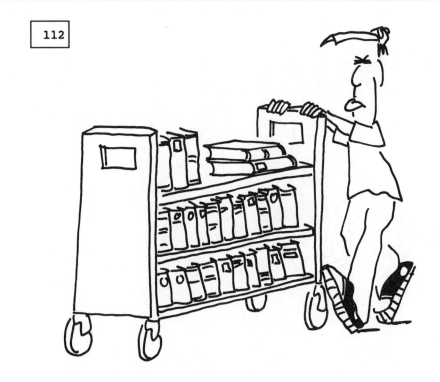

Then it happened. I had to shelve
a book in the sports section, when
I discovered the baseball books. I
found all my heroes. I found the
history of the game. I found
statistics. And it was painless!

My Story

Then I found books on baseball cards. I found out how much they were worth. I love baseball cards, and I could be rich. I wouldn't even have to go to spring training! Suddenly I loved the library.

Dad was happy. Mom was happy.
And I was happy knowing that if I
stayed working at the library, I
could afford tons and tons of
baseball cards! I was going to be
one rich librarian!